SECURITY IS A THUMB AND A BLANKET

BY CHARLES M. SCHULZ

First paperback edition 1971
Revised, expanded paperback edition 1983
Reprint of revised, expanded paperback edition 1990

Based on "Security is a Thumb and a Blanket"
by Charles M. Schulz

Published by Determined Productions, Inc.
Box 2150, San Francisco, CA 94126
Printed in Hong Kong

ISBN 0-915696-79-7
Library of Congress Catalog Card No. 82-70029

The first edition of **SECURITY IS A THUMB AND A BLANKET,** written and illustrated by world-famous cartoonist Charles M. Schulz, appeared in 1963. Its immediate success followed the lead of the first best seller, HAPPINESS IS A WARM PUPPY.

Now the beloved PEANUTS® characters are back in a new, enlarged version of **SECURITY IS A THUMB AND A BLANKET.** You'll find the familiar blend of Schulz nostalgia and humor, but three times as many pages of cartoons and sentiments, all in color. Snoopy and the entire PEANUTS® gang will warm your heart — again!

You'll also want to ask for the new and enlarged versions of HAPPINESS IS A WARM PUPPY, LOVE IS WALKING HAND-IN-HAND, I NEED ALL THE FRIENDS I CAN GET, CHRISTMAS IS TOGETHER-TIME **and** HOME IS ON TOP OF A DOG HOUSE.

Security is an album of happy memories.

Security is knowing someone will help you with your homework.

Security is a good watchdog.

Security is
never having
to eat lunch
by yourself.

Security is
learning to do
the things that are
expected of you.

Security is finding a new friend at camp.

Security is
a friend who isn't
embarrassed
when you cry.

Security is
a dressmaker who
understands you.

Security is growing your own vegetables.

Security is
an experienced
pilot.

Security is
keeping
the ol' body
in shape.

Security is
riding
on the back
of your
mom's
bike.

Security is following a leader.

Security is being on a team with professionals.

Security is getting a lot of valentines.

Security is being first in line at the movies.

Security is a naturally dazzling smile.

Security is knowing all the steps.

Security is
a pair
of warm,
woolly socks.

Security is being a member of the club.

Security is
knowing someone
who wants
to put you on a
pedestal.

Security is having "wheels."

Security is
having friends
you can trust.

Security is a well-stocked cupboard.

Security is
learning
not to be afraid.

Security is
never missing
a cue.

Security is
a good
secretary.

Security is
something
that helps you
stay afloat.

Security is
a new recipe book
for the cook.

Security is understanding an "in" joke.

Security is
being one
of the gang.

Security is
a good tan.

Security is being the doctor instead of the patient.

Security is
knowing people
who like
houseguests.

Security is
three sharp pencils
and lots
of erasers.

Security is
an umbrella.

Security is believing in statehood, countryhood, cityhood and neighborhood.

Security is
a friend
with a
swimming
pool.

Security is
not having
to eat out
alone.

Security is believing in the Great Pumpkin.

Security is knowing where you can get a pizza after midnight.

Security is
having friends
in high places.

Security is
a good
alarm system.

Security is
one thing to one person
and another thing
to another person.

Security is
a full book
of phone
numbers.

Security is
having a friend
who likes to talk
on the phone
as long as
you do.

Security is a strong backhand.

Security is
having a friend
who knows
the answers.

Security is
knowing there'll
be someone
to catch you
if you fall.

Security is
a thumb
and a
blanket.

Security is
taking advantage
of every
opportunity.

Security is practicing sand shots.

Security is
fastening
your
seat belt.

Security is
not having to worry about where you'll get dinner.

Security is having someone to lean on.

Security is
scarfing
fresh cookies
in front of a
warm TV.

Security is
being smothered
with kisses.

Security is
having a friend
who'll screen your
phone calls.

Security is
a night light.

Security is having a list when you go Christmas shopping.

Security is flight insurance.

Security is not having to worry about tomorrow.